The small business is the way to escape the rat race and be your own boss. As you expand you can be the boss of a growing business. I did it, it's fun, hard work and frustrating all in one.

This book shows you how to deal with negative feedback in an efficient manner.

eBay: 10

SIMPLE STEPS
TO REMOVING
NEGATIVE
FEEDBACK
2015

A Guide to Removing Negative
& Neutral Feedback from eBay

ISBN 9781507722268

Contents

Acknowledgements

I am deeply grateful to have around me friends, family, colleagues and Customers. This book came from their assistance.

I am deeply grateful in particular to my wife Janat without whom none of this would have been possible,

Introduction

Have you ever bought or sold an item on eBay? If so, you've probably stumbled across a seller feedback rating. Feedback ratings vary in purpose, from ensuring the credibility of the seller to verifying the level of service provided.

If you sell items on eBay regularly, you are most likely very aware of your feedback ratings and overall feedback score. Although reputable sellers most often receive positive feedback, there are some situations in which a negative or neutral feedback score may be awarded after a transaction. Regardless of the circumstances that cause this to occur, it is important to know what defences you have at your disposal to move forward and continue a productive relationship with your eBay clients.

After authoring numerous books and creating various YouTube videos on the topic, I decided it was important to address more thoroughly how to handle these situations. What follows is a detailed guide on how to mitigate negative feedback on eBay, effectively removing its effect on your account (and your business).

1

What is Negative Feedback?

The process begins when a customer places an order on eBay. After each transaction, every customer is afforded the option to indicate their opinion on a number of factors:

Item as described – does your item match its description?

Communication – how well you communicate with the buyer

Dispatch time – how quickly you send the item and how long the mail takes

Postage and Packaging Charges – How you charge for postage and packaging

Each feedback item falls into one of three categories: positive, negative and neutral. Future customers are then able to utilise this feedback to determine whether or not they want to do business with the seller. There are different categories and qualifiers used by eBay in the rating of each. By selecting different levels of performance, the seller is awarded one of the aforementioned categories of feedback.

It all sounds very simple, doesn't it? But when the number of regular eBay users and transactions is taken into account, it can seem overwhelming to manage the feedback process. In this regard, it is important for you to remember that the goal of feedback is simply to rate the seller, taking into account each aspect of the sale.

With that in mind, let's talk about how an eBay sale works.

2

Anatomy of an eBay Sale

At the beginning of every sale is a product. Typically, when running an eBay-based business, the seller purchases items to place on eBay from their suppliers (assuming that the sale is in the form of "order fulfilment" rather than "drop shipping" – more clarification on that in a moment. For the average item, the seller takes an appealing photograph of the item, determines what will motivate the customer to purchase the item solving their problem, and crafts a high quality description to encourage a potential buyer to make a purchase. After all this is complete, the item is loaded on eBay. Check how many photographs that you can see on eBay taken in a bathroom or with a terrible background.

The key to this is to ensure that this process is done correctly. The seller should treat each item equally, working through the process carefully to ensure that their item is attractive to potential customers and solves the problem that they have.

As for the other transaction details, a few components are included: cost of shipping, locations the seller is willing to ship to, and any other defining items. The four most important parts, however, are the photograph, item description, item quality (new or used) and postage whether first or second class. By shipping free, it gives you a higher rating on eBay.

3

The Next Step: Selling the Item

Putting an item on sale creates a listing that is visible to anyone, anywhere. Potential buyers can view the item and consider purchasing it. Naturally, browsers or "window shoppers" are simply looking around, whereas regular customers are typically attracted to items that are of the best quality with good feedback.

After an item is up for sale, it can take a while before a buyer is found. Typically, patience is a requirement to do business on eBay. Get it right, and you will have a huge amount of sales. You have 6 seconds to attract a buyer to even look at your page so make it good. Finally, however, a buyer purchases the item. Once payment is completed, the seller receives an e-mail congratulating them on the transaction. At this point, depending on the technical savvy of the seller, they may have a program in place that automatically issues feedback for the buyer. This is a great opportunity to send some positive feedback with a marketing message, in order to develop an on-going relationship with the customer.

Now, it is time for the seller to neatly wrap up the item and ship it to the buyer. After the shipping process is complete, the buyer will receive the item and, although it may seem odd, this is the first critical moment for the seller's feedback rating. The first impression that your item makes is essential to ensuring that you get a great rating. Your item should be neatly wrapped, tidily packaged and the address label should have leading capitals on the name and address. Your customer's first thoughts will be: "Is this the right item?" and "Does the quality match the description?" Get this right, and you may receive an instant positive feedback.

I have been with people who have bought items from eBay and other e-commerce sites. The packaging has been awful. They are pleased to have received their item but dismayed at the state of the packaging. It is such a disappointment to receive a package that looks awful. I ordered an item from eBay, and when it eventually arrived, my address was taped to the envelope. The address was written on a piece of paper that had been torn from the corner of a sheet of paper. It looked terrible. It was so bad that I ordered it again. The same envelope turned up again. I wrote to the seller no reply.

How would you like to receive this? When you post an order to a buyer, just ask yourself how you would like to receive this. One person who sells on eBay told me it did not matter – as long as they get their order, they don't care what it looks like. This person had a lot of people claiming not to have received their order and a lot of negative feedback. I worked with them to tidy up their postal supplies, and a lot of their problems disappeared.

Your goal throughout this process should be to delight the customer in order to receive a positive feedback rating. Another important component is your responsiveness to customer issues; if you receive a complaint from the customer, you should work quickly and effectively to make things right. Otherwise, you may be subjecting yourself to negative feedback and a dispute with eBay's customer support. To avoid this, be both polite and helpful when contacted. Professional interactions go a long way in avoiding negative and neutral feedback. Always thank the Customer for their valued order and no matter how fed up you are with the Customer, always be polite and courteous. I have received e-mails from Customers that were awful. Some of their comments are 'if you can be bothered to reply'. Regardless of a Customer's comment, always reply as a professional, keeping your standards very high. Do not blame someone else. Better to assume responsibility and apologise for the problem. It goes down far better than blaming everyone but you. How many times do you hear big companies blaming everyone else for their shortcomings? I have lost count of the number of times I have been quoted, "I am so sorry." They are nothing of the sort and do not really mean what they say. They read this from a script and say it with no feeling.

This brings us to our next point – how do you handle customer service with an order that is drop shipped?

4

Drop Shipping vs. Order Fulfilment

In short, the difference between Drop Shipping and Order Fulfilment is this: in cases of order fulfilment, the seller has possession of the product, packages it, and ships it to the customer. Conversely, in a drop shipped order, the seller is a middleman. They arrange for the entity (usually a wholesale company) that possesses the item to send it directly to the customer. For example, imagine you want to sell garden furniture. You could find a good product through a wholesaler's e-commerce site that might cost £200 when you order in a quantity of 1 - 3 items. You know that each item would likely sell on another e-commerce site for £300, so you list the item on eBay at £290. By doing so, you have a competitive price and are more likely to sell the item; furthermore, you're making a profit of £90. At this point, there are two options for you as the seller. You can either fulfil the order yourself – meaning you would order the item from the wholesaler, have it shipped to your inventory space (be it your home, office or warehouse), and then reship the item to the customer. In this case, what I refer to as order fulfilment, you would retain the profit less the shipping cost. Alternatively, upon selling the item, you can take the data received from the buyer and input their details in your wholesale order. The customer then receives the product, and you keep all of the profits. This would be an instance of drop shipping.

Now, drop shipping obviously sounds like the easier of the two paths; however, there are a few problems. First and foremost, your financial return may be lower than that in the example described, meaning that you'll have to fulfil a lot of orders to make a decent profit.

Second, you are depending on the reliability of a potentially unknown vendor for the satisfaction of your customer. If, for example, your vendor notifies you that they are out of stock **AFTER** you have sold the item to your customer, then you have a problem. You have a customer that expects to receive the product and no way of getting it to them. In this case, you may have to purchase the item from another wholesaler that charges more, cutting into your profits. Or you may have to cancel the order if there is no more stock.

Finally, if the item is running late, you will have to reach out to the vendor and find out where the item is and how long they expect it to be delayed. In cases like these, you may end up with an unhappy customer; however, as always, problems like these can usually be managed with high-quality customer service.

In some cases, you simply can't make a customer happy. In times like these, it's important to have a process established for how you're going to handle the situation.

5

Creating Your Process

It may seem self-explanatory, but a process is something that you develop over time to carry out a set of tasks. In the case of a business, it's important to reflect on your business model and ideals, and to come up with your own best practices to manage a variety of situations. As with anything else, the best way to test your processes is to use them. Then, as your business develops over time, your processes will evolve to suit your needs better. By doing this, you'll begin to uncover the very best ways to handle any situation your business might throw at you.

Developing your processes will not occur overnight; however, you will typically find that, in the long run, your processes are beneficial to your business and will result in a methodology that produces the results you want. That's how I started and ended up with my current processes for handling negative and neutral feedback that delivers great results almost every time.

6

Negative Feedback: Your First Reaction

Imagine it: you're just starting out with your new e-commerce business. You've had a few great sales with wonderful, positive feedback. Everything is going along smoothly … and then it happens. A customer leaves you negative feedback for the first time.

When I first started doing business on eBay and received my first piece of negative feedback, I panicked. I was sure my business was over and had no idea what to do. After calming down somewhat, I took the first logical step – like any new user would, I contacted eBay's customer support to figure out my options.

eBay was very helpful in this situation and provided some basic support. They offered some suggestions on how to repair the situation and gave a bit of advice. I took a deep breath and began following the steps they provided (a huge step toward creating our process for handling negative feedback). Still, it was a nerve-wracking two hours as I tried to contact our customer and have the negative feedback removed.

7

How to Handle Negative Feedback

The process that I established includes the following:

1. Carefully read the negative feedback and try to work out what the problem is. It is not always obvious, but it's important to take this first step. That way, you can approach the customer armed with an understanding of what upset them or what they are trying to achieve. Sometimes you will have no idea. Typically having bought an item and left negative feedback with no prior communication with the seller.

2. The first rule of handling feedback – neutral or negative – is to be polite and professional. No matter how irritating negative feedback may be, writing a damning reply like, "This is an evil buyer, do not touch with a barge pole," is not going to help your situation. Why? Because your customers expect you to be professional; if they see you responding negatively to other customers, they may not buy from you. You have to keep your business going.

3. Reply to the feedback. Craft your reply based on what you sell and where you are, but always start with thanking the customer for their feedback. The first goal of this reply is to calm down your upset buyer, not to encourage any additional negativity. In some cases, your customers may even be so surprised by your gratitude for their feedback that they are interested in having a discussion with you.

4. Always check to see if the customer is a fellow seller on eBay. It's often amazing how big an impact the "same team" approach (i.e., "We're both business people and we both rely on great feedback to do business") can turn negative feedback from another eBay seller around.

5. An important next step is to carefully review the feedback for defamatory words like "fake." In cases like these, where the wording of the feedback can be highly detrimental to your future sales, it's important to contact eBay immediately and address the situation. eBay has a defamation form that can be used to object in cases where the customer's feedback might negatively impact your reputation in an on-going way. To access the defamatory form go to the search facility. Type in Claim and the defamation form will appear. Fill it in, it's fully self-explanatory, and submit it. You define it as a legal document.

6. Write a message to the buyer who left you feedback (again, remembering to be polite and professional). Here's an example:

> "Dear <customer>,
>
> Thank you for your order and your feedback.
>
> We were shocked by your negative feedback and that your order was not to your satisfaction and would like to see if we can resolve the situation to meet your needs. We value your opinion and hope to hear from you soon.
>
> Kind Regards,
> <You>"

Again, it is critical to thank the customer for their order and their feedback, ensuring that they feel like a valued part of the business. From there, I can go on to discuss a resolution to the situation. What I *haven't* done however in my response is mention the negative or neutral feedback removal. It's important to address any concerns from their feedback (i.e. "The item arrived late") in your initial message. This assures the customer making them feel that they are being listened to. From there, you can establish an open dialogue with the customer and begin to repair/build your relationship.

7. Contact eBay. An important component of this call is to remain just as polite and professional as you would with a customer; in short, no launching into tirades regarding your negative feedback. Treating your customer service representative with respect can be very helpful in handling any situation. The effect of this can be amazing, especially since most people who contact eBay support are upset and inconsiderate toward the representative.

8. Discuss your negative feedback. Give them the background of the situation and explain any important details. This is different from rambling. The first question your eBay support representative will ask is, "Have you contacted the buyer?" In this case, if you follow this process, the answer is YES. From there, you can certainly ask the representative to remove the feedback – after all, nothing ventured yields nothing gained. Sometimes the representative may ask to place you on hold; if they do, be sure to remain polite and wait patiently while they investigate your case. If they remove the negative feedback, be sure to thank them and wish them a nice day. Do the same even if they do not remove the negative or neutral feedback.

After speaking to eBay's support services, there are two more important tasks in your process:

9. Block the buyer from purchasing more of your items. After all, regardless of the situation and the result, you don't want to deal with a customer that is quick to leave negative feedback.

10. Report the buyer to eBay. The simplest explanation for this is that eBay's Trust and Safety department receives plenty of single complaints about buyers; however, if your customer service representative reported your situation, there will be a trend established for that buyer. This way, you are protecting yourself and your fellow sellers in the event that this person is up to no good.

Finally, I advise that you contact the buyer again within a few hours and again if necessary. In many cases, the buyer will respond to your messages, but not always. If they do reply, it's important to be responsive to any additional needs that they may have. This will contribute to a positive on-going relationship. If, however, the customer continues to be negative or abusive, then it's time to contact eBay again.

If the buyer does respond and is open to discussion, it's important to open a dialogue about what you can do to improve their satisfaction with their purchase. Negotiating with a dissatisfied buyer can be tricky, but people are often reasonable, and a solution can typically be found without too much trouble. I have had many buyers who have said I did not mean to leave negative feedback. I have encountered buyers who if they have a problem leave a negative feedback just so that you contact them. Once you have made contact and sorted the problem, the negative feedback is removed.

After you've resolved the customer's concerns, it's time to ask the buyer if they agree to revise their neutral or negative feedback being revised. In some cases the buyer may suggest this. To send a request to revise negative or neutral feedback follow these steps. At the bottom of the eBay Web page. There is a site map selection. Select the Site Map, look for the feedback area and the select the button labelled "Request Feedback Revision" – this shows the list of feedback you can send a revision about. Select the appropriate one, give the reason for changing the feedback and press send. This sends a request to the customer to revise their feedback. In some cases, you may need to send a gentle reminder to the buyer after a day or two, to ensure that they complete the feedback revision. The buyer changes the feedback from a negative or neutral feedback to a positive feedback. Be warned do not use this unless the buyer has agreed to revise the feedback. Alternatively, especially in cases where there may be a language barrier between you and the customer, you can ask them to send you a message giving their permission for the negative feedback to be removed. You can then follow up with your eBay support representative to handle the situation.

Hopefully, this process can guide you through removing any negative or neutral feedback; it isn't guaranteed to work, but it is a good place to start. Handling negative feedback isn't always easy, but it is always worth it. After all, we're talking about your reputation! The main thing is it shows that you are a professional seller. I have found little impact on my sales after a negative feedback with using this technique.

8

Positive Mental Attitude

One of the most powerful things I have found throughout this process is to have a Positive Mental Attitude. Not only do you always look on the bright side of life, but being positive all the time has the effect of keeping you in a positive frame of mind. You will be more creative and be far more positive than if you wrote an e-mail to a person who had left you negative feedback in a bad mood. In fact, if you are moody, grumpy, annoyed or just in a bad mood, just leave the comment on the negative or neutral feedback and don't follow up until you have calmed down. By adding a polite and logical comment, you are helping protect your future sales.

How many footballers do you see walk up to take a penalty only to blast it over the bar? The reason is that they have taken the penalty saying to themselves, *do not miss do not miss*. The only thing in their mind is not to miss. What do they do? Miss. Your aim is always to avoid negative feedback, and if you get one, to aim to get the negative feedback removed.

When you get that negative or neutral feedback, it's not the end of the world, even though it may feel that way. Keep yourself positive and work towards resolving the situation with positive results.

9

Examples: Cases of Negative Feedback

What follows are several cases of customers who have left negative feedback on my account. Hopefully, these cases will provide a useful example of how to successfully manage feedback and can teach you something new to improve your own process for handling negative feedback.

Case #1

I had a customer purchase an item from me, after which I heard nothing for three weeks. Then I suddenly received a notification of negative feedback for the transaction. It read: "Item arrived late and broken." I followed our established process and replied to the feedback. However, the customer didn't appear to be very nice. In fact, further investigation revealed that they had feedback from other sellers, calling them a "thief" and suggesting not selling to them. This was a slight confidence booster, but after speaking with eBay, I learned there wasn't much they could do at the moment since the feedback was so vague.

I reached out to the customer again and eventually received a reply. The buyer stated, "the item had not arrived for three weeks and, when it arrived, it was smashed to bits. There was glass everywhere. I had to throw it in the bin since I have a child."

First, I would like to note that this is impossible, since the item was sealed in polythene and glass couldn't have escaped the packaging; however, in cases like these, it is critical to remember that the best course of action is to remain professional and polite. eBay is almost always going to take the side of the customer, so when I called again with this new information, I wasn't surprised that eBay said there was still nothing they could do. Our support representative recommended that I continued to speak with the buyer in order to reach a resolution.

After contacting the buyer and reiterating our apologies for the late and damaged order, I agreed to refund their money from the transaction in return for removal of the negative feedback. The customer agreed, and I refunded their money, only to have the negative feedback left on our account. I contacted other sellers that the buyer had purchased from and discovered that this had happened several times recently. This was truly educational on how hard it can be to keep your account free of negative and neutral feedback, as I did everything in our power to make the buyer happy and I am still left with negative feedback on the transaction. I did later get the negative feedback removed after contacting eBay again having gathered more evidence.

Case #2

The next case was especially hard to deal with because it occurred soon after I started doing business on eBay. I was very inexperienced, and this particular case made it difficult to trust future customers.

I sold several items to a customer and received an e-mail about one of the items being faulty. I asked the buyer to return the items to us; however, they wrote and informed us that they were disabled and unable to leave the house to ship the item back since they were bedridden.

Being a compassionate business person, I said that we would replace the item and shipped it to the customer. A week later, I received an e-mail that said, "I have been to the shop that sells your product. They have informed us that all of your products are fake, if you do not give us a full refund I am going to leave negative feedback on your account." Obviously they had magically got better very quickly.

First and foremost, nothing I sell is fake. Beyond that, I had never experienced anything like this before. Later, I learned that this is called "feedback extortion," but at the time it was frightening. Furthermore, you can imagine the effect this would have on your ability to believe claims made by future customers. It's because of this case that I learned to ask that complaints be supplemented with photographic evidence; however, you never forget the first experience like this one.

Case #3

In another situation with negative feedback, I sold and shipped four items to a new customer. Shortly after the items arrived, I received an e-mail stating that the package had only contained one item.

Now, in our case, I mark each package with different codes to indicate how many items are contained inside. Codes like this are useful for inventory management and ensuring order accuracy, as well as handling customer complaints. I asked the customer to photograph the items and the packaging, but they refused.

As soon as the customer refused to send us a photo, I suspected there might be a problem. In cases where the customer has a legitimate complaint, they are often more than happy to send proof. I attempted to question the customer a bit further, to no avail. At that point, the customer opened a case with eBay.

I replied to the case, asking for the items to be returned in exchange for a refund. The customer then claimed to have already sent the items back through the courier (PayPal) and that the tracking number was the case number. I received negative feedback and replied, as per our process. After a week, I hadn't received the items and contacted eBay – the case was closed, and the negative feedback was removed.

In this situation, I learned just how hard it can be to have negative feedback removed, but that patience and perseverance will often be rewarded.

Case #4

This has to be my favourite instance of negative feedback ever. I sold an item to a customer and, within three days, had received a message that the item had been received with a crack in it. I was sceptical at first, because these items are hard to break, and the customer's description of the crack seemed unlikely based on the object's design.

Another unusual component of the complaint was that the initial message contained photographs of the item, showing the crack. Typically, I don't receive photographic evidence until I ask for it, which made this situation a bit bizarre. I continued to ask some questions, like if they knew how the item had been broken, but received only guarded and vague responses. It was at this point that I truly felt there was something fishy going on. When I asked the customer to return the item for a refund/replacement, they refused.

The customer indicated that the cost of returning the item to the UK was EUR 30. Even when I offered to pay the postage, the customer was unwilling to ship it back. Finally, I went back to the packaging and asked for a photo of the envelope. The customer again declined our request. They claimed that the item hadn't been wrapped properly – that there was no tape on the bubble wrap, and the item had been lying loose in the envelope.

Knowing I would never send an item like that, I confirmed our suspicions when I referred to the original photographs. I discovered that the bubble wrap for the item was in the background of the photo **with** tape still on it. Furthermore, I enhanced the photograph to discover that the crack was actually just a line drawn with a pencil – it started and stopped on the surface of the plastic and showed no cracking in the body of the item.

I reported back to the customer with our findings and kindly requested that they either return the item or drop their complaint. The buyer then threatened to open to open a case and simultaneously gave us negative feedback, claiming that the item had arrived cracked. I replied to the feedback politely and professionally, and went back to eBay to handle the case. I was informed that the customer had indicated that they were content to use the broken item and that eBay was unable to remove the feedback.

Case #5

Our next buyer was incredibly savvy at using the eBay feedback system. The customer ordered an item and, after receiving it, sent an e-mail indicating that the item was not what they had ordered. The customer had listed three sellers in the message, because they had purchased several items and weren't sure which one had arrived incorrectly. I asked for a picture of the item and a photograph of the envelope, which the customer provided. I acknowledged the photos, and it was all downhill from there. It seems I had been selected as the guilty party, so I proceeded to handle the case.

The customer sent a photograph of the item, claiming I had sent the wrong one. Unfortunately, the photograph they sent was of an item that was both used and not something that I sell. I informed the customer of these points – politely and professionally, as always – and said I wasn't able to help them. At this point, I received multiple messages threatening an open case and negative feedback; however, I didn't back down, knowing that I could prove I didn't stock or sell that item. The next day, negative feedback was posted, and a transaction dispute was opened through PayPal. I contacted both eBay and PayPal the same day, and they removed the feedback and closed the dispute case.

In situations like these, customers can sometimes get it into their heads that the seller doesn't have any recourse against a complaint; however, with proper documentation and a good business process, you can avoid these types of disputes.

Case #6

Our final case study is simply a testament to the nature of some people. I sold an item to a customer and sent the item out via unregistered post. Several days later, the customer opened a case and claimed they hadn't received the item and left negative feedback. I contacted them and agreed to send a replacement.

This time, I sent the item via registered post. At this point, I moved on. Shortly thereafter, I received an e-mail stating that the customer had escalated the case through eBay and was claiming they still hadn't received the item. I checked on the registered post and, lo and behold, the item had never been signed for. Needless to say, the case ended up in the customer's favour.

A few days later, I continued to monitor the registered post and, as if by magic, the item was received and signed for. I contacted eBay immediately and never heard anything more about the case, and the feedback was removed.

10

Conclusion

If you're anything like I was when I first started, you're not sure how to handle negative feedback. You may not even understand the impact that negative feedback has on your sales. The best advice I can give is to practice good customer service from the start to, hopefully, avoid receiving negative feedback in the first place. That said, at the end of the day, there will always be instances where you receive negative feedback.

As these examples may demonstrate, the process for successfully handling negative feedback doesn't always work. Sometimes I experienced success and sometimes I didn't. But what the process can do is provide a foundation and some best practices to go by to help minimise the impact that negative feedback has on your business. Handling this part of your business is difficult, but by being responsive, polite and professional, you can manage your account well and build your reputation to help your business. I hope that this information helps.

Some buyers will give you negative or neutral feedback and never remove it. No matter what you do. By replying to the neutral or negative feedback, you provide a professional approach that often gives potential buyers confidence in you. I have tonight just received a negative and a neutral feedback. I have followed the process and the sales have never slowed down.

Good luck and happy eBaying.

Thank you for reading my book. I hope that you have enjoyed it. I would welcome any feedback you may have by contacting me on Linkedin, you can find me at uk.linkedin.com/in/theebayguy

I look forward to hearing from you

www.ingramcontent.com/pod-product-compliance
Lightning Source LLC
Chambersburg PA
CBHW070744180526
45168CB00004B/1525

* 9 7 8 1 5 0 7 7 2 2 2 6 8 *